INTERACTIONS I
A Listening/Speaking
Skills Book

SECOND EDITION

INTERACTIONS I
A Listening/Speaking
Skills Book

Judith Tanka
University of California, Los Angeles

Paul Most

McGraw-Hill, Inc.
New York St. Louis San Francisco Auckland Bogotá
Caracas Lisbon London Madrid Mexico City Milan
Montreal New Delhi San Juan Singapore
Sydney Tokyo Toronto

This is an book

Interactions I
A Listening/Speaking Skills Book
Second Edition

7 8 9 0   DOH DOH   9 5 4 3

ISBN 0-07-557528-0

Cover illustration: **Rufino Tamayo** *Wedding Portrait (Retrato matrimonial),* 1967. Oil on canvas, 136 x 195 cm. B. Lewin Galleries/Palm Springs, California.

Sponsoring editor: Eirik Børve
Developmental editor: Mary McVey Gill
Project editor: Marie Deer
Copyeditor: Stacey Sawyer
Art director: Jamie Sue Brooks
Text and cover designer: Cheryl Carrington
Illustrators: Axelle Fortier and Sally Richardson
Typesetter: Graphic Typesetting Service
Printer and binder: R. R. Donnelley & Sons Company

To our parents

CONTENTS

PREFACE TO THE SECOND EDITION

Interactions: The Program

INTERACTIONS consists of ten texts plus two instructor's manuals for in-college or college-bound nonnative English students. INTERACTIONS I is for high-beginning or low-intermediate students, while INTERACTIONS II is for low-intermediate to intermediate students. Within each level, I and II, the books are carefully coordinated by theme, vocabulary, grammar structure, and, where possible, language functions. A chapter in one book corresponds to and reinforces material taught in the same chapter of the other three books at that level for a truly integrated, four-skills approach.

Each level, I and II, consists of five books plus an instructor's manual. In addition to the listening/speaking skills books, they include:

A Communicative Grammar I, II: Organized around grammatical topics, these books include notional/functional material where appropriate. They present all grammar in context and contain a wide variety of communicative activities.

A Reading Skills Book I, II: The selections in these books are written by the authors and carefully graded in level of difficulty and amount of vocabulary. They include many vocabulary building exercises and emphasize reading strategies: for example, skimming, scanning, guessing meaning from context, understanding the structure and organization of a selection, increasing reading speed, and interpreting the author's point of view.

A Writing Process Book I, II: These books use a process approach to writing, including many exercises on pre-writing and revision. Exercises build skills in exploring and organizing ideas, developing vocabulary, using correct form and mechanics, using coherent structure, editing, revising, and using feedback to create a final draft.

A Speaking Activities Book I, II: These books are designed to give students the opportunity to practice their speaking and listening skills in English by promoting realistic use of the language through individual, pair, and small-group work. Task-oriented and problem-solving activities simulate real-life situations and help develop fluency.

Instructor's Manual I, II: These manuals provide instructions and guidelines for use of the books separately or in any combination to form a program. For each of the core books except *Speaking Activities,* there is a separate section with teaching tips, additional activities, and other suggestions. The instructor's manual also includes sample tests for the grammars and readers.

The grammatical focus for the twelve chapters of *Interactions I* is as follows:

1   the simple present tense; pronouns
2   the present continuous tense vs. the simple present; *there* vs. *it*; the modals *can, may, might, will*
3   nouns; comparison of adjectives and adverbs; the modals *can, could, will, would, may*; the future with *be going to*
4   review; phrasal verbs
5   the simple past tense; *used to*
6   the past continuous tense; infinitives
7   more on infinitives; *should, had better,* and *must*; the reflexive; adjective clauses with *who* and *that*
8   review
9   the present perfect with *since, for*; the present perfect continuous
10   gerunds
11   the present perfect tense with *just, already, yet, still,* and so forth; the superlative
12   review

Interactions I: A Listening/Speaking Skills Book

When listening to English, lower-level students have two basic needs:

1. to understand the essence of messages beyond their level; i.e., day-to-day comprehension for survival and
2. to learn effective listening strategies which, in turn, will lead to language acquisition itself.

Whereas traditional emphasis in lower-level listening texts has typically been on testing comprehension, *Interactions I: A Listening/Speaking Skills Book* is concerned with teaching high-beginning or low-intermediate students *how to listen.*

Chapter Organization

Organized around a theme, each chapter is divided into four listening strategies and a speaking section:

Part One   Getting the Main Idea; Stressed Words and Reductions

1. As students listen to an introductory conversation, they actively focus on the stressed words that signal important information.
2. Students learn to recognize and reproduce reduced forms common in spoken American English.

Part Two   Summarizing Main Ideas

Students identify and pick out relevant details from a short corpus of information—e.g. messages, announcements, etc. Then, based on their notes, students reconstruct the message either orally or in writing.

Part Three   Making Inferences

Students use contextual clues to understand implied messages in a conversation. Since the answers to the questions appear later in the conversation itself, students get the benefit of immediate feedback.

Part Four   Listening Tasks

In this section students demonstrate their comprehension by performing practical tasks involving material such as drawings, maps, and application forms.

Part Five   Speaking Activities

Role-plays, small-group activities, and class discussions complement the listening component. These speaking activities are natural extensions of the chapter theme and offer imaginative opportunities to further explore it.

Teaching Hints

The philosophy behind this book is to teach students listening skills that will help them "see the forest from the trees" in their complex listening environment— i.e., the real world. Consequently, the exercises will seem quite challenging. While the exercises themselves aren't extremely complicated, they do heavily depend on the students' full understanding of the instructions and goals. Therefore, we recommend that teachers spend sufficient time clarifying the purpose and method of each exercise prior to assigning it.

For further specific teaching guidelines, consult our instructor's manual.

Changes to the Second Edition

1. There are new pronunciation exercises and other new listening exercises as needed.
2. A variety of new speaking activities were added, including an activity called "Cartoon Skits" (a role-play) for every chapter.
3. Idioms and useful expressions are listed at the beginning of each chapter.
4. Answers to exercises are included in the instructor's manual.

Recommendations for Testing

Listening comprehension is not a skill that can be improved through the memorization of rules or discrete items. For this reason, progress in listening comprehension is not easy to test. Generally, we do not recommend giving students grades in listening since it is not something they can take home and study. However, if the teacher must give grades and tests, we recommend using chapters from the book for this purpose.

We have found almost no teachers who cover all twelve chapters of the text in one course or semester, even in intensive programs where students have listening every day. In most cases there is enough material in the book that two, and possibly even three, chapters could be used as tests. Chapter 6, for example, could be used as a midterm and Chapter 12 as a final exam.

For the purpose of testing, using existing chapters with their accompanying tapes is particularly useful for foreign-born teachers, who may have accents that make it awkward for them to give oral tests in which they read the material to the students.

If a quantitative score is required, a percentage could be obtained by counting the number of blanks (or questions) that the student fills in (or answers) correctly and dividing that number by the total number of blanks (or questions). This would be quite laborious, however, as the book was designed for the purpose of teaching, not testing. An easier method of grading would be to use pluses, checks, and minuses; or, easiest of all, to grade holistically.

Regardless of the grading method used, we recommend that students receive a different "grade" for each section of the chapter because each section tests a different aspect of the student's listening ability.

Finally, we recommend that the teacher not start giving grades until Chapter 3 at the earliest, as we have seen that students need to work through the first two chapters in order to become accustomed to the format of the book.

Ancillaries

1. Audiocassettes, to be used in conjunction with the student book
2. Instructor's manual
3. Tapescript

Acknowledgments

Of the many people who in various ways helped us complete this book, we would especially like to thank the following: Elaine Kirn, our colleagues at UCLA, and Mary McVey Gill and the staff of McGraw-Hill.

Thanks also to the following reviewers of the first edition for their help on the second edition: Anne Bonemery, James Burke, John Kopec, Linda Levine, Laurie Roberts, Jenise Rowekamp, and Christine Salica.

J. T.
P. M.

INTERACTIONS I
A Listening/Speaking
Skills Book

1

SCHOOL LIFE

Idioms and Useful Expressions in this Chapter

You will hear the following expressions in this chapter. If you are not sure what they mean, try to guess the meanings from the context.

How are you doing?	Call me at 555-4940.
Stop by anytime.	Give me a call.
Can you give us an idea of . . . ?	Pick it up.
a snack bar	a midterm exam
a gym	What's the make of your car?
a T.A.	
a chem class	
a math class	

PART ONE

GETTING THE MAIN IDEAS: STRESSED WORDS AND REDUCTIONS

A. Jack, Tom, and Herb are new students at Faber College. They meet in the student lounge of their rooming house. Listen to the conversation. You may not understand every word. Listen for the main ideas.

B. Listen again. The important words are "stressed"; these words give the main idea.

Example: My name is Tom.

Write the following stressed words in the correct places:

hi	right	Tom Riley	Herb	meet	accent
doing	name	Tom	hi	from	you're
Jack	Tom	roommate	Herb	Texas	accent

JACK: _____ ! How are you _____ ?

TOM: Oh, hi! You're _____ , right?

JACK: That's _____ . What's your _____ again?

TOM: _____ . _____ _____ .

JACK: _____ , this is my _____ _____ .

TOM: _____ , _____ .

HERB: Nice to _____ you.

TOM: Where are you _____ ?

HERB: _____ .

TOM: Oh, yeah, you have an _____ !

HERB: Ha! _____ the ones with the _____ !

C. Now listen again. Repeat each sentence after the speaker. Remember that stressed words are *louder* and *clearer* than unstressed words.

3

D. Now listen to the rest of the conversation. Underline the stressed words.

> JACK: <u>Listen</u>, <u>Tom</u>. We're <u>really hungry</u>. Do you <u>want</u> to get <u>something</u> to <u>eat</u> with us?
> TOM: I can't. I have to meet my new roommate, Kenji. I think he's Japanese.
> HERB: Okay. See you later, then. We're up in 212. Stop by anytime.
> TOM: Hey, we're on the same floor. Room 220.

E. Listen again. Notice the stressed words.

F. Listen to the following questions. You will hear each question twice. Write the answers.

1. _____

2. _____

3. _____

4. _____

5. _____

6. _____

7. _____

G. **Reductions.** Important words are usually stressed. Many words that are not stressed are "reduced"—for example, *do you > doya, how are you > how're ya*. Listen to these examples of reductions from the conversation. Repeat them after the speaker.

Reduction*	Long Form
Hi! <u>How're ya</u> doing?	Hi! How are you doing?
Tom, <u>this's</u> my roommate Herb.	Tom, this is my roommate Herb.
Nice to <u>meetcha</u>.	Nice to meet you.
<u>Where're ya</u> from?	Where are you from?
<u>D'ya wanna</u> get something to eat with us?	Do you want to get something to eat with us?
I have <u>ta</u> meet my roommate, Kenji.	I have to meet my roommate, Kenji.

*The underlined forms are not acceptable spellings in written English.

H. You will hear a few sentences. Write the missing words.

1. _____ _____ _____ feeling?

2. _____ _____ in an hour.

3. Jack, _____ _____ _____ _____ eat at the cafeteria?

4. When _____ _____ _____ _____ meet your roommate?

I. Pronunciation of the -s ending. The -s ending has three pronunciations.†

1. /s/   drinks, speaks
2. /iz/   teaches, uses
3. /z/   carries, brings

Listen to the following words. Check the sound you hear.

	/s/	/iz/	/z/
1. plays			✓
2.			
3.			
4.			
5.			
6.			
7.			
8.			

J. Answer the following questions in complete sentences. Pay attention to the -s endings.

1. Where does your teacher work?
2. What does he or she teach?
3. Does your teacher give you homework?
4. When does your class begin?
5. When does it end?

---

†1. Pronounce the ending as an /s/ sound after a /p/, /t/, /k/, or /f/ sound.
 2. Pronounce the ending as an added syllable after an /s/, /z/, /sh/, /ch/, or /j/ sound.
 3. Pronounce the ending as a /z/ sound after other consonant and vowel sounds. It is not an added syllable.

PART TWO

SUMMARIZING THE MAIN IDEAS

A. Listen to the following speech. You will not understand every word. Think about these questions:

1. Who is speaking?
2. Who is listening to the speech?
3. Where are they?

B. Did the speaker say the following?

Welcome to Faber College.	yes	no
Faber is a great school.	yes	no
We hope you like it.	yes	no
A campus tour begins in fifteen minutes.	yes	no

C. If you answered *yes* to all statements, you understood the *main* or *important* ideas. Remember: You don't need to understand all words to understand the main message.

D. Listen to the full speech again. Focus on the main ideas only.

E. One of the students asks the tour guide this question: "Can you give us an idea of some good places to eat?" Listen to the answer to her question. Write the important key words. The answer has two parts.

Part A, key words: _____

_____

Part B, key words: _____

_____

F. Listen again to each part. Summarize each part in short, simple sentences. Use your key words. This is not a dictation. Do not copy every word.

Part A: _____

_____

_____

_____

_____

_____

Part B: _____

_____

_____

_____

_____

_____

_____

PART THREE

MAKING INFERENCES†

Listen to the conversation among Jack, Tom, and Kenji. Circle the answer to each question you hear. Then listen to the next part of the conversation. It gives you the correct answer.

1. a. at a horse race
    b. at the bookstore
    c. at a pizza restaurant

2. a. another student in their class
    b. a waiter
    c. the teaching assistant in their chemistry class

3. a. It's a little unusual.
    b. It's terrible.
    c. It's fun.

4. a. at the recreation center only
    b. on the telephone
    c. by paying $5

5. a. He is sure he and Kenji will win.
    b. He is sure they will lose.
    c. He is not ready.

---

†An *inference* is a guess or an assumption; you make an *inference* from other
information or evidence.

PART FOUR

LISTENING TASKS

A. Tom and Kenji have a message machine. When they are not home, it tape-records telephone calls for them. Listen to the people who call. Are they friends? Classmates? Parents? What do they call about? Who gets more messages, Tom or Kenji? Why? Complete the form for each message with the important information. Listen to the example:

TELEPHONE MESSAGE:

For _Kenji_

Caller _Dr. Brown_

Phone _855 - 7962_

        Area Code Number Extension

☐ Telephoned   ☑ Please call back

☐ Returned your call   ☐ Will call back

Message: _Change appointment from Tues. → Wed. 2:00_

1.

```
TELEPHONE MESSAGE:

For _____

Caller _____

Phone _____
        Area Code   Number   Extension
☐ Telephoned        ☐ Please call
                       back

☐ Returned your     ☐ Will call back
  call

Message: _____

_____

_____
```

2.

```
TELEPHONE MESSAGE:

For _____

Caller _____

Phone _____
        Area Code   Number   Extension
☐ Telephoned        ☐ Please call
                       back

☐ Returned your     ☐ Will call back
  call

Message: _____

_____

_____
```

3.

```
TELEPHONE MESSAGE:

For _____

Caller _____

Phone _____
        Area Code   Number   Extension
☐ Telephoned        ☐ Please call
                       back

☐ Returned your     ☐ Will call back
  call

Message: _____

_____

_____
```

4.

```
TELEPHONE MESSAGE:

For _____

Caller _____

Phone _____
        Area Code   Number   Extension
☐ Telephoned        ☐ Please call
                       back

☐ Returned your     ☐ Will call back
  call

Message: _____

_____

_____
```

5.

TELEPHONE MESSAGE:

For _____

Caller _____

Phone _____
        Area Code   Number   Extension

☐ Telephoned   ☐ Please call
                           back

☐ Returned your ☐ Will call back
   call

Message: _____

_____

_____

6.

TELEPHONE MESSAGE:

For _____

Caller _____

Phone _____
        Area Code   Number   Extension

☐ Telephoned   ☐ Please call
                           back

☐ Returned your ☐ Will call back
   call

Message: _____

_____

_____

7.

TELEPHONE MESSAGE:

For _____

Caller _____

Phone _____
        Area Code   Number   Extension

☐ Telephoned   ☐ Please call
                           back

☐ Returned your ☐ Will call back
   call

Message: _____

_____

_____

B. Herb calls the college about a parking permit and talks to a secretary. Listen to their conversation and complete the application.

PARKING PERMIT APPLICATION

Faber College

Name: _____
       Last   *First*   *Middle Initial*

Address: _____

Phone: _____

Car: _____
     Make   *Model*   *Year*

License Plate: _____

Fall Quarter ☐

Winter Quarter ☐

Spring Quarter ☐

All year ☐

PART FIVE

SPEAKING ACTIVITIES

A. Group work. Write your first name on a card and put it on your desk for everyone to see. Sit in a circle, if possible. Ask another student three or four questions to find out something about him or her.

Examples: Where are you from? What do you do? Do you work? Do you have a hobby?†

Now introduce that student to other students.

Examples: José, this is Noriko. Noriko, this is José.
José, I'd like you to meet Noriko. Noriko, I'd like to introduce José.

Then put away your name cards. Go around the room and see how many names you remember. There are various ways to find out someone's name.

Examples: Excuse me, what's your name again?
I'm sorry, can you tell me your name again?
I'm sorry, I don't remember your name.
You're Noriko, right?

B. Discussion. In Part I, Jack introduces Herb to Tom. Look at the drawings and tell what "body language" they use. Do they look directly at each other? Do they stand far apart? Now tell what these gestures mean in America. Are they the same in your culture?

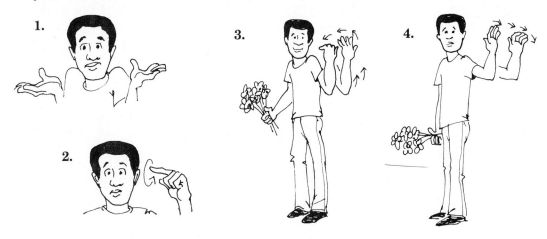

---

†When you meet someone for the first time, don't ask him or her about money
("How much is your rent, salary, etc.?"), age ("How old are you?"), or religion
("What is your religion?").

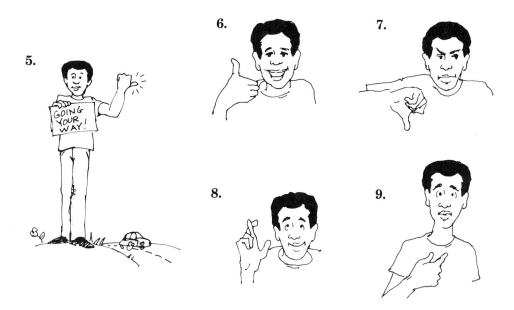

C. Use body language to show the following situations.

1. You don't know the answer to a question.
2. Tell your friend that the class is boring.
3. You can't hear what someone says.
4. Someone on the phone is talking too much.

D. Cartoon skits. Joe and Naomi are first-year students at the same college. They meet for the first time when their bicycles collide. What do they say? How do they feel? Will they meet again?

Prepare a conversation with a partner. Use expressions and idioms from this chapter. Then put on a skit about the situation.

2

NATURE

Idioms and Useful Expressions in this Chapter

You will hear the following expressions in this chapter. If you are not sure what they mean, try to guess the meanings from the context.

The weather is going to clear up.
What's the weather like?
I'm worn out.
lows
mid-fifties
highs
The weather is going to warm up.

I don't mind (the heat).
What's it like out?
I think I'll pass. (No, thanks).
How was the weather?
Celsius (Fahrenheit)
It's 13 below.
in the high (low) seventies

PART ONE

GETTING THE MAIN IDEAS: STRESSED WORDS AND REDUCTIONS

A. Tom, Herb, and Mike are going away for the weekend. Listen to their conversation in the car. You may not understand every word. Listen for the main ideas.

B. Listen again. Write the following stressed words in the correct places:

real	hate	traffic	raining	think
bad	nothing	winter	kinds	summer
cowboys	dry	egg	funny	skiing
snows	hot (use twice)			

14

TOM: I _____ to drive in _____ like this.

MIKE: Especially when it's _____ .

HERB: You _____ this is _____ ? Back in Texas a little rain like this is _____ !

TOM: Really? Isn't Texas _____ and _____ ?

HERB: Oh, we have all _____ of weather in Texas. In the _____ it's so _____ you can fry an _____ on the street. And in the _____ it _____ in some places.

MIKE: Well, you never see pictures of _____ _____ .

HERB: Ha-ha! _____ _____ .

C. Now listen again. Repeat each sentence after the speaker. Remember that stressed words are *louder* and *clearer* than unstressed words.

D. Now listen to the rest of the conversation. Underline the stressed words.

MIKE: Boy, this road is narrow. Be careful! We don't want to spend the week in the hospital.

HERB: So, when do you think we'll get to Bald Mountain?

TOM: Not before midnight.

HERB: Then let's stay in a motel tonight.

TOM: Yeah, it doesn't look like the weather is going to clear up.

MIKE: And I'm not going camping in the woods until I hear the weather report.

E. Listen again. Notice the stressed words.

F. Listen to the following questions. You will hear each question twice. Write the answers.

1. _____

2. _____

3. _____

4. _____

5. _____

6. _____

7. _____

G. Reductions. Listen to these examples of reductions from the conversation. Repeat them after the speaker.

Reduction*	Long Form
We 'ave all kinds o' weather in Texas.	We have all kinds of weather in Texas.
When d'ya think we'll get to Bald Mountain?	When do you think we'll get to Bald Mountain?
We don't wanna spend the week in the hospital.	We don't want to spend the week in the hospital.
It doesn't look like the weather is gonna clear up.	It doesn't look like the weather is going to clear up.

*The underlined forms are not acceptable spellings in written English.

H. You will hear a short conversation. Write the missing words.

PETE: What _____- _____ _____ in the car?

GAIL: We _____ all kinds _____ stuff.

PETE: _____ _____ _____ any drinks?

GAIL: Sure. What _____ _____ _____ _____ have?

PETE: How _____ _____ Coke?

I. Intonation. Notice the difference in intonation between these two sentences:

I can meét you tomorrow.

I can't meét you tomorrow.

Can is not stressed. *Can't* is stressed.
Listen and repeat these sentences. Then circle *yes* if the statement is affirmative. Circle *no* if the statement is negative.

1. yes	(no)	6.	yes	no
2. yes	no	7.	yes	no
3. yes	no	8.	yes	no
4. yes	no	9.	yes	no
5. yes	no	10.	yes	no

PART TWO

SUMMARIZING THE MAIN IDEAS

A. Tom, Mike, and Herb are at a motel. They see a man and a woman talking to the manager. The man and the woman look tired but excited. Listen to their story.†

B. Now listen again. You will hear parts of the same conversation. Write short sentences using the following words. Don't try to write everything. Just take notes and try to get the main ideas of the story.

1. we / camp / nearby

_____

2. we / get / back / camp

_____

3. want / dry / clothes

_____

†Sometimes in English, people use the simple present tense to tell a story about the recent past.

4. into / tent

    _____

5. tent / mess

    _____

6. only / clothes / missing

    _____

7. outside / look / around

    _____

8. see / bears

    _____

9. bears / wear / clothes

    _____

C. Now listen to the same story in simple form. Compare your nine sentences with what you hear.

PART THREE

MAKING INFERENCES

Tom, Mike, and Herb are camping in the woods. Listen to their conversation. Circle the answers to each question you hear. Then listen to the next part of the conversation. It gives you the correct answer.

1. a. He is fishing.
    b. He is cooking a fish.
    c. He is telling a secret.

2. a. They're hungry.
    b. They're angry.
    c. They're tired.

3. a. It's enjoyable.
    b. It's uncomfortable
    c. It's boring.

4. a. to the top of a mountain
    b. to a place for lunch
    c. to the valley

5. a. Shoot a gun.
    b. Take photographs.
    c. Send postcards.

PART FOUR

LISTENING TASKS

A. Mike is listening to the weather forecast on the radio. Take notes about the weekend's weather.

	FRIDAY	SATURDAY	SUNDAY
Sky (clear? cloudy? fair?)	_____	_____	_____
Temperature			
High	_____	_____	_____
Low	_____	_____	_____
Rain (yes? no?)	_____	_____	_____

B. Listen to the following conversations about the weather. Write the key words that help you know what season it is. Then write the name of the season.

1. Clues: _nice surprise, usually cooler, brown leaves_

   Season: _____

2. Clues: _____

   Season: _____

3. Clues: _____

   Season: _____

4. Clues: _____

   Season: _____

C. Listen to the conversations about the weather. Circle the temperature you hear.

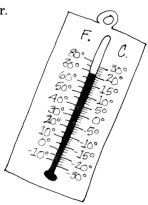

1. 19   95   99
2. 80   18   8
3. 13   30   30s
4. 14   40   44
5. 103   130   133
6. 30s   30   13
7. −13   30   3
8. 70   70s   17

PART FIVE

SPEAKING ACTIVITIES

A. **Pair work.** What activities do you think about when you think of winter? Spring? Summer? Fall? Look at the chart about New York. Ask your partner about the weather and activities in New York during different seasons.

Example: What's the weather like in New York during the spring?
              What sport is popular in the fall?

Then think about your home country or city. Fill in the second chart. Explain it to a partner from a different country.

UNITED STATES: NEW YORK

	Jan., Feb.	*Mar., Apr., May*	*June, July, Aug.*	*Sept., Oct.*	*Nov., Dec.*
	WINTER	SPRING	SUMMER	FALL	WINTER
Weather	cold snow rain cloudy/grey	warm/cool rain	hot/humid sunny	cool windy rainy	cool/cold rain/snow
Things to Do	ski skate	plant flowers walk, bike ride	go to beach swim travel school vacation picnic barbecue	walk in park	skate walk in park
Sports	hockey		baseball	football	football
Major Holidays	New Year's Day Presidents' Day	Easter	Memorial Day Fourth of July	Labor Day Columbus Day	Thanks- giving Christmas

YOUR COUNTRY: _____

	Jan., Feb.	*Mar., Apr., May*	*June, July, Aug.*	*Sept., Oct.*	*Nov., Dec.*
	WINTER	SPRING	SUMMER	FALL	WINTER
Weather					
Things to Do					
Sports					
Major Holidays					

B. Group work. Sit in small groups. Choose one of the sports below. Describe the sport but don't mention its name. Let the other students guess which sport you are talking about. Use *can* and *can't* with the correct stress.

Example: You can do this sport in all seasons, but it's more popular in the summer. Most children can do it, but sometimes it can be dangerous. You can do it outdoors or indoors, and you don't need any special equipment, just a bathing suit. You can do it by yourself, but you can't do it outside the water!

When each person in the group has chosen a sport, describe other sports that you know about.

C. **Cartoon skits.** It seldom rains in Los Angeles. But Bernie is a careful man; he always carries an umbrella. And today he's glad. But what about the others?

In groups of three, prepare a conversation. Use expressions and idioms from this chapter. Then put on a skit about the situation.

3

LIVING TO EAT OR EATING TO LIVE?

Idioms and Useful Expressions in this Chapter

You will hear the following expressions in this chapter. If you are not sure what they mean, try to guess the meanings from the context.

a grocery list
a checkbook
an express line
groceries
a sale

a fast-food place
a barbecue
on sale
for sale
a shopping cart

PART ONE

GETTING THE MAIN IDEAS: STRESSED WORDS AND REDUCTIONS

A. Mr. and Mrs. Nutley, an elderly couple, are in the supermarket on a Saturday afternoon. Listen to their conversation. You may not understand every word. Listen for the main ideas.

B. Listen again. Write the following stressed words in the correct places:

why	always	cents	things	strawberries
that	grocery	aren't	army	shopping
do	nice	cookies	hungry	have (twice)
fresh	see (twice)	like		

24

MR. N: Well, dear, I _____ a few _____ that _____ on the _____ list.

MRS. N: I can _____ _____ ! You're not _____ for an _____ , you know.

MR. N: You know I _____ _____ this when I'm _____ .

MRS. N: Well, let's _____ what you _____ here.

MR. N: Some _____ , _____ _____ for only ninety-nine _____ .

MRS. N: Well, that's okay. But _____ do you have all these _____ ?

MR. N: I don't know; don't you _____ them?

C. Now listen again. Repeat each sentence after the speaker. Remember that stressed words are *louder* and *clearer* than unstressed words.

D. Now listen to the rest of the conversation. Underline the stressed words.

> MRS. N: Oh, I suppose. I hope you have a box of soap here.
> MR. N: Sure—a large one.
> MRS. N: That steak looks really expensive!
> MR. N: Well, it isn't. It's just three dollars a pound.
> MRS. N: What's this? More ice cream? We already have a gallon at home. Put it back and hand me my checkbook.
> CASHIER: I'm sorry, ma'am; this is the express line. You have too many groceries, and we don't take checks here.

E. Listen to the following questions. You will hear each question twice. Write the answers.

1. _____

2. _____

3. _____

4. _____

5. _____

6. _____

7. _____

F. **Reductions.** Listen to these examples of reductions from the conversation. Repeat them after the speaker.

Reduction*	Long Form
Let's see whatcha have here.	Let's see what you have here.
Why d'ya have all these cookies?	Why do you have all these cookies?
I dunno.	I don't know.
Doncha like 'em?	Don't you like them?

*The underlined forms are not acceptable spellings in written English.

G. You will hear a short conversation. Write the missing words.

> CUSTOMER: Waiter!
>
> WAITER: Yes, sir. Do you know _____ _____ want?
>
> CUSTOMER: _____ _____ have any fresh whitefish?

WAITER: Yes, we catch _____ fresh every day.

CUSTOMER: Great, I'll have some.

WAITER: What kind of wine _____ _____ want with that?

CUSTOMER: I _____ _____ . Why _____ _____

recommend something?

WAITER: Our California wines are excellent.

H. Intonation: Teens or tens? Notice the differences in stress between the following pairs of words. In the numbers thirteen to nineteen, stress the syllable *-teen* as well as the first syllable. For 20, 30, 40, etc., to 90, stress the first syllable only.

thirtéen   thírty   fourtéen   fórty   eightéen   éighty

Listen to these sentences. Write the numbers you hear.

PART TWO

SUMMARIZING THE MAIN IDEAS

A. Kenji and his friends are shopping at Shop-and-Save Department Store. They hear some announcements. Before you listen, think about what kind of things stores announce to their shoppers—for example, special sales, locations, store hours, etc.

B. Now listen again. Write the important information. Don't copy sentences. Just take notes:

New hours: _____

Special sale: _____

Sportswear: _____

Parking: _____

Little boy: _____

C. Write your own short announcement for each important point.

_____

_____

_____

_____

_____

_____

_____

_____

_____

_____

_____

_____

_____

_____

_____

_____

PART THREE

MAKING INFERENCES

Listen to each of the following conversations. In each, decide where the people are eating and circle the answer. Then listen to the next part of the conversation. It gives you the correct answer.

1. a. coffee shop
   b. cafeteria
   c. nice restaurant

2. a. fast food place
   b. coffee shop
   c. expensive restaurant

3. a. cafeteria
   b. nightclub
   c. fast-food place

4. a. nice restaurant
   b. cafeteria
   c. fast-food place

PART FOUR

LISTENING TASKS

A. Tom is teaching Kenji how to cook. Listen to the recipe for French toast and take notes on it.

Ingredients: _____

_____

_____

1.

2.

3.

Steps:

1. Beat _____

2. Melt _____

3. Dip _____

4.

5.

4. Fry _____

5. Serve _____

B. Mr. and Mrs. Nutley plan to drive around the United States soon. Their niece, Paula, is a chef. She tells them about foods popular in different parts of the country. Take a look at the map of the United States and Canada. As you hear the names of different foods, write them on the map in the places where they are popular.

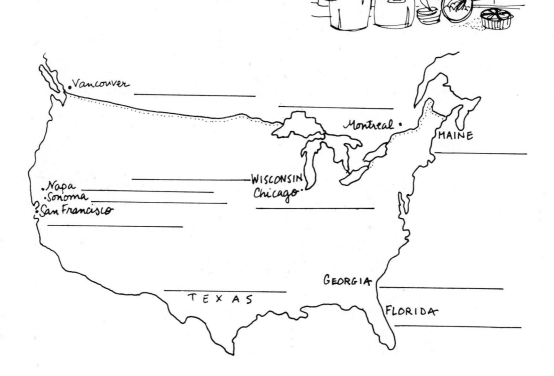

PART FIVE

SPEAKING ACTIVITIES

A. **Group work.** For this activity, the class is in two groups. Group A should look only at List A and cover List B. Group B should look only at List B and cover List A.

Look at your list. It's different from the other group's list. These are things you need for a typical American barbecue. What does the other group have? Ask questions. Try to find all the things on the other group's list.

Examples: Group A member. Do you have any onions?
Group B member: No, we don't have any.
Group A member: Do you have some ketchup?
Group B member: Yes, we have a bottle.

LIST A

Supplies	*Food*
plates	potato chips
plastic cups	hot dogs
charcoal	chicken
_____	green salad
_____	mustard
_____	watermelon
Beverages	_____
Coke	_____
beer	_____
coffee	_____
ice	_____
_____	_____
_____	_____
_____	_____

LIST B

Supplies	*Food*
plastic knives, forks, etc.	cheese
napkins	hamburgers
matches	buns
_____	potato salad
_____	ketchup
_____	ice cream
Beverages	cake
iced tea	_____
wine	_____
juice	_____
_____	_____
_____	_____
_____	_____

B. Discussion. Look at the drawings and compare shopping at a supermarket with shopping at a small stand.

Example: large, good-looking
Where are the tomatoes larger and better-looking?
Tomatoes are larger and better-looking at the stand.

1. cheap: _____

2. ripe: _____

3. fresh: _____

4. crowded: _____

5. modern: _____

6. friendly: _____

7. convenient: _____

Now discuss the following questions:

1. Which place has lower prices? Can you guess why? _____

_____

2. Whose food is fresher? Why? _____

_____

3. Which place is cleaner? _____

_____

4. Which is a nicer place to shop? Why? _____

_____

C. Class presentation. Teach your class a simple recipe from your country. First list the ingredients. Then describe each step. Use Exercise A in Part Four as a model.

D. Cartoon skits. Cathy is expecting dinner guests tonight. She has found everything she needs at the supermarket. She is ready to pay, but . . . what happened to her wallet?

Prepare a conversation with one or two partners. Use expressions and idioms from this chapter. Then put on a skit about the situation.

4

GETTING AROUND THE COMMUNITY

Idioms and Useful Expressions in this Chapter

You will hear the following expressions in this chapter. If you are not sure what they mean, try to guess the meanings from the context.

to get a haircut	How long does it take?
to get around	turn right (left)
to get on	How do I get there?
to get off	make a right (left)
a dry-cleaning shop	

PART ONE

GETTING THE MAIN IDEAS: STRESSED WORDS AND REDUCTIONS

A. Herb and Mike live in a small college town near a big city. Mike needs to go into the city today. Listen to their conversation. You may not understand every word. Listen for the main ideas.

B. Listen again. Write the following stressed words in the correct places:

might	traffic	give	like	sure
bad	package	much	around	what
bank	can't	back	things	help
math	take	city	taxi	

HERB: Say, Mike. Can you _____ me some _____ with my

_____ homework this afternoon?

34

MIKE: Umm, I'd _____ to, but I really _____ . I have to go

into the _____ and do a lot of _____ .

HERB: Like _____ , for example?

MIKE: I have to go to the _____ and open a checking account, I have to

mail a _____ at the post office, and I _____ get a

haircut, too.

HERB: Well, that's not _____ . When are you going to come

_____ ?

MIKE: I'm not _____ . I might eat downtown if the _____ looks

_____ .

HERB: How are you going to get _____ ?

MIKE: I think I'll _____ a _____ .

C. Now listen again. Repeat each sentence after the speaker. Remember that stressed words are *louder* and *clearer* than unstressed words.

D. Now listen to the rest of the conversation. Underline the stressed words.

HERB: Take the bus; it's much cheaper.
MIKE: Maybe I will. Can I get you anything?
HERB: Could you get me some stamps?
MIKE: Sure.
HERB: And would you buy me some tennis balls?
MIKE: . . . Okay.
HERB: Oh, yeah . . . and our camping pictures are ready. Pick them up, if you can.
MIKE: Is that all, boss?
HERB: Yes, for now.

E. Listen again. Notice the stressed words.

F. Listen to the following questions. You will hear each question twice. Write the answers.

1. _____
2. _____
3. _____
4. _____
5. _____

G. Reductions. Listen to these examples of reductions from the conversation. Repeat them after the speaker.

Reduction*	Long Form
Kin ya gimme some help?	Can you give me some help?
I'd like ta, but I can't.	I'd like to, but I can't.
I have ta go into the city and do a lotta things.	I have to go into the city and do a lot of things.
When are ya gonna come back?	When are you going to come back?
How're ya gonna get around?	How are you going to get around?
Can I getcha anything?	Can I get you anything?
Couldja get me some stamps?	Could you get me some stamps?
And wouldja buy me some tennis balls?	And would you buy me some tennis balls?
Pick 'em up if you can.	Pick them up if you can.

*The underlined forms are not acceptable spellings in written English.

H. You will hear a short conversation. Write the missing words.

ANA: _____ _____ show me where the bus stops?

SUE: _____ _____ _____ , but I really don't know.

You'll _____ _____ ask someone else. Or I can

_____ _____ some bus maps.

ANA: Forget it; you're _____ _____ be late.

SUE: No, I don't _____ _____ rush.

ANA: Okay. _____ _____ please get _____ , then?

SUE: Sure, I'll _____ _____ right up.

ANA: _____ _____ bring an extra for my friend?

PART TWO

SUMMARIZING THE MAIN IDEAS

A. Mike is back after a long afternoon in the city. He looks tired and unhappy. Listen to his conversation with his friends.

B. Now listen again. List the good things and the bad things you hear about cities and towns.

GOOD THINGS
+

BAD THINGS
—

Big Cities

GOOD THINGS	BAD THINGS
1. _____	1. _____
2. _____	2. *noise*
3. *good shopping*	3. _____
	4. _____
	5. _____
	6. _____

Small Towns

GOOD THINGS	BAD THINGS
1. *quiet*	1. *conservative*
2. _____	2. _____
3. _____	

C. Now tell in your own words the good things and bad things about big cities and small towns. Use your notes. Make complete sentences.

Example: Life in a big city is more expensive than in a small town.

_____

_____

_____

_____

_____

_____

_____

_____

_____

_____

_____

_____

_____

PART THREE

MAKING INFERENCES

Listen to each of the following conversations in the city. Circle the answer to the question you hear. Then listen to the next part of the conversation. It gives you the correct answer.

1. a. in a post office
    b. in a bank
    c. in a gas station

2. a. on a train
    b. in a taxi
    c. on a bus

3. a. at a clothing store
    b. at a dry-cleaner's
    c. at a coffee shop

4. a. getting a driver's license
    b. visiting the eye doctor
    c. taking a final exam

5. a. at the airport
    b. at a bank
    c. at a post office

PART FOUR

LISTENING TASKS

A. Mike is getting directions to various places in the city. Right now he is at Joe's Diner on Columbus Street. Look at the map and follow the directions you hear. Write the *name* of *each place* where Mike goes in the correct place on the map.

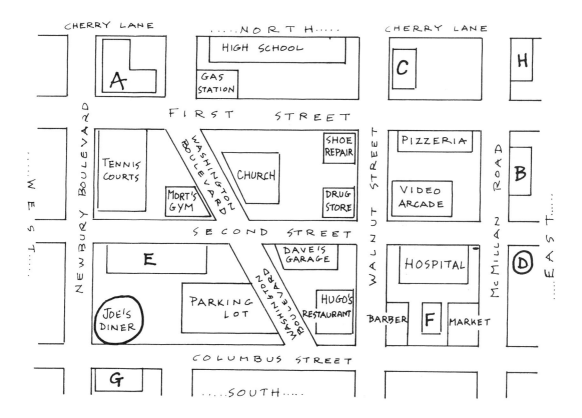

B. If you need directions, your local bus company can help you. Just tell them where you want to go, from where you want to leave, and what time you need to go. Listen to the following telephone conversations with the Metro Bus Company. Take notes on each conversation.

1. Destination: _____

    Bus number: _____

    Get on at: _____   Time: _____

    Get off at: _____   Time: _____

2. Destination: _____   Times: _____

    Get on at: _____   _____

    Fare: _____

    Travel time: _____

3. Destination: _____

    Bus number: _____

    Get on at: _____

    Get off at: _____

    Bus runs: _____

PART FIVE

SPEAKING ACTIVITIES

A. Pair work.

1. Look at the map in Part IV. Work with a partner. Ask for directions to a number of places on the map.

    QUESTION: How do I get from the park to the gas station?

    ANSWER: Go south on McMillan, turn right on First Street, and you'll see the gas station on the corner of First and Washington Boulevard.

2. Describe your neighborhood to a partner. Use *there is, there are, it's*.

    Example: My neighborhood is noisy but it's safe. There's a movie theater near my house. It's about three blocks from me.

B. Discussion. Tell about various types of transportation in your hometown and where you live now. Are people dependent on one form of transportation? (Do they have only one?) How do you like to get around? By bus? By car? By taxi? On foot? Explain why and in what situations.

C. Cartoon skits. Mr. Kim was in a hurry to buy a surprise birthday present. When he finished shopping, he got a surprise himself!

Prepare a conversation with a partner. Use expressions and idioms from this chapter. Then put on a skit about the situation.

5

HOUSING AND THE FAMILY

Idioms and Useful Expressions in this Chapter

You will hear the following expressions in this chapter. If you are not sure what they mean, try to guess the meanings from the context.

It was a real pain.   to share a house
Wow!   a leaking faucet
Everything is a mess.
I bet . . .
That's too bad

PART ONE

GETTING THE MAIN IDEAS: STRESSED WORDS AND REDUCTIONS

A. Tom and his friends are waiting for Mike at a restaurant. Listen to their conversation. You may not understand every word. Listen for the main ideas.

B. Listen again. Write the following stressed words in the correct places:

hour	five	waited	were	did
say	out	moved	corner	apartment (twice)
decided	had	without	sorry	why
where	old	sister (twice)		

TOM: So where _____ you? We _____ for an _____ , but then we _____ to have lunch _____ you.

MIKE: _____ , guys. I _____ to help my _____ move _____ of her _____ _____ .

TOM: _____ you _____ your _____ just _____ ?

MIKE: Yeah.

TOM: _____ was her _____ ?

MIKE: Right around the _____ . Just _____ minutes away. _____ ?

C. Now listen again. Repeat each sentence after the speaker. Remember that stressed words are *louder* and *clearer* than unstressed words.

D. Now listen to the rest of the conversation. Underline the stressed words.

> TOM: My friend Barbara needs a place right away. How big is it?
> MIKE: It's a one-bedroom apartment with a small kitchen and bathroom. The living room has a fireplace.
> TOM: Great! What did she pay there?
> MIKE: Only four-fifty, but it might go up.
> TOM: Could you give me the address for Barbara?
> MIKE: Sure. Tell her to see the manager soon, before it's rented.

E. Listen again. Notice the stressed words.

F. Listen to the following questions. You will hear each question twice. Write the answers.

1. _____

2. _____

3. _____

4. _____

5. _____

6. _____

7. _____

G. **Reductions.** Listen to these examples of reductions from the conversation. Repeat them after the speaker.

Reduction*	Long Form
Didja say your sister moved?	Did you say your sister moved?
I had ta help.	I had to help.
She had ta get out.	She had to get out.
I' was only four-fifty.	It was only four-fifty.
Couldja gimme the address?	Could you give me the address?
Tell 'er to see the manager.	Tell her to see the manager.

*The underlined forms are not acceptable spellings in written English.

H. You will hear a short conversation. Write the missing words.

A: _____ _____ get your new phone yet?

B: Yeah, but I _____ _____ call the phone company three times.

It was a real pain. Here's my new number. When you see Jane, _____

_____ _____ _____ my number, too?

I. Pronunciation of the -ed ending. The *-ed* ending has three pronunciations.†

1. /id/   waited, invited
2. /t/   fixed, watched
3. /d/   lived, showed

Listen to the following words. Check the sound you hear.

	/id/	/t/	/d/
1. turned			✓
2.			
3.			
4.			
5.			
6.			
7.			
8.			
9.			

J. Answer the following questions with complete sentences. Pay attention to the *-ed* endings.

1. When did you move to this city?
2. Who recommended this school to you?
3. When did you start learning English?
4. When did you call your family?
5. When did you brush your teeth?

---

†1. Pronounce the ending as an added syllable after a /d/ or /t/ sound.
2. Pronounce the ending as a /t/ sound after a /p/, /k/, /s/, /sh/, /ch/, or /f/ sound.
3. Pronounce the ending as a /d/ sound after other consonant and vowel sounds.

PART TWO

SUMMARIZING THE MAIN IDEAS

A. Barbara is looking at Marsha's old apartment. Listen as the manager shows Barbara around the apartment.

B. Listen again. Take notes about the good things and the bad things about the apartment.

GOOD THINGS	BAD THINGS
1. *new paint*	1. _____
2. _____	2. _____
3. _____	3. _____
4. _____	4. *higher rent*
5. _____	5. _____
6. _____	6. _____

PART THREE

MAKING INFERENCES

Mike's sister Marsha also found a new place to live. Listen to Mike and Marsha's conversation. Circle the answer to each question you hear. Then listen to the next part of the conversation. It gives you the correct answer.

1. a. coffee
   b. magazines
   c. a pack of cigarettes

2. a. in the living room
   b. outside the house
   c. in the bedroom

3. a. It's very large.
   b. It isn't large.
   c. He couldn't find the bedroom.

4. a. a friend
   b. a dog
   c. a baby

5. a. because the rent was high
   b. because the rent was low
   c. because the rent was late

PART FOUR

LISTENING TASKS

A. Barbara moved. She is at the post office. A clerk is helping her fill out a change-of-address form. Listen to the conversation.

Listen again and complete the form with the information you hear.

Print or Type *(Last Name, First Name, Middle Initial)*		
OLD ADDRESS	No. and St., Apt., Suite, P.O. Box or R.D. No. (In care of)	
	Post Office, State and ZIP Code	
NEW ADDRESS	No. and St., Apt., Suite, P.O. Box or R.D. No. (In care of)	
	Post Office, State and ZIP Code	
Effective Date		
Sign Here ▶		

Signature & title of person authorizing address change (DO NOT print or type)

B. It's moving day. Look at Barbara's empty new apartment. Listen to her instructions to the movers.

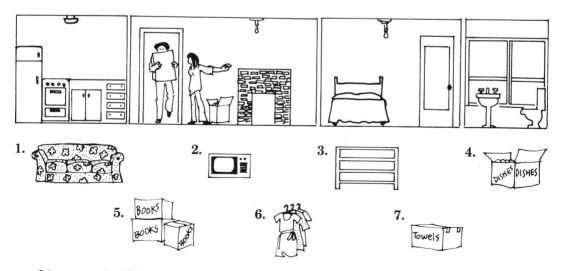

1.   2.   3.   4. DISHES DISHES

5. BOOKS BOOKS BOOKS   6.   7. Towels

Listen again. This time write the number of the item in the correct place on the picture.

C. Mr. Nutley passes Barbara on his way into his apartment. Listen to their conversation. Now listen again and take notes.

Information about Mr. Nutley: _____

_____

The neighborhood seventeen years ago: _____

_____

_____

The neighborhood now: _____

_____

_____

Use your notes to retell what you heard on the tape.

PART FIVE

SPEAKING ACTIVITIES

A. Role play. Here are three apartment ads; they do not give very much information. Make up at least five questions to ask the manager.

1.

| Beautiful apartment; walk to campus. Call 555-2009 for more information. |

Rent? _____

Number of rooms? _____

Noise? _____

Stove/refrigerator? _____

? _____

2.

| Two-bedroom apartment. $500. Good location. Call 555-1828. |

Area? _____

Lease? _____

Garage? _____

Number of bathrooms? _____

? _____

3.

> Roommate needed to share house. Lots of privacy. Leave message at 555-5520.

Male/female? _____

Number of rooms? _____

Smoking? _____

Location? _____

Rent? _____

Now work with a partner. One of you is the manager, and the other one wants the apartment. Use your prepared questions. Change roles for each ad.

B. Group work. Look at the pictures and tell a story about Marsha's moving day. Use the verbs below the pictures. Use the past tense and pronounce the endings carefully. The story continues on the next page.

Example: Marsha **moved** into her house and **paid** the movers. Then she **remembered.**

1.

move

2.

pay

3.

remember, call

4.

look

5.

unpack

6.

wash, drop

7.

dust

8.

paint

9.

plant

10.

rest

C. **Cartoon skits.** Ali's rent just went up, so he wants to share his apartment with someone. Roberto wants to move out of his parents' house and is looking for a cheap place to live. They meet at "Roommate Finders."

Prepare a conversation with a partner. Use expressions and idioms from this chapter. Then put on a skit about the situation.

6

EMERGENCIES AND STRANGE EXPERIENCES

Idioms and Useful Expressions in this Chapter

You will hear the following expressions in this chapter. If you are not sure what they mean, try to guess the meanings from the context.

to help out   to be lost
Oops!   hijacking

GETTING THE MAIN IDEAS: STRESSED WORDS AND REDUCTIONS

A. Listen to the following conversation on the tennis court. You may not understand every word. Listen for the main ideas.

B. Listen again. Write the following stressed words in the correct places:

tried	leg	fell	happened	scream
wrong	knee (twice)	where	broken	net
doctor	hurt	help	excuse	playing

TOM: Nice game, guys!

HERB: Oops . . . Ow—my _____ !

TOM: What's _____ ? _____ does it _____ , Herb?

HERB: My _____ . I think it's _____ .

DOCTOR: _____ me, can I _____ ? I'm a _____ . I was _____ over there when I heard you _____ . What _____ ?

HERB: I _____ to jump over the _____ and I _____ on my _____ .

C. Now listen again. Repeat each sentence after the speaker. Remember that stressed words are *louder* and *clearer* than unstressed words.

D. Now listen to the rest of the conversation. Underline the stressed words.

DOCTOR: Can you move it?

HERB: Yeah, but it really hurts.

DOCTOR: Okay, now try to stand up. I'll help you. Good. Well, it's not broken, although it'll probably hurt for awhile. Don't plan to play any more tennis this week.

TOM: Is it a good idea to put some ice on his knee?

DOCTOR: Yes, and it's important to lie down with your leg up while you're doing that.

TOM: We're lucky you're here. How can we thank you?

DOCTOR: Oh, I'm always happy to help out. But if you want to give me a tennis lesson sometime . . .

E. Listen again. Notice the stressed words.

F. Listen to the following questions. You will hear each question twice. Write the answers.

1. _____

2. _____

3. _____

4. _____

5. _____

6. _____

7. _____

G. Reductions. Listen to these examples of reductions from the conversation. Repeat them after the speaker.

Reduction*	Long Form
I tried <u>ta</u> jump over the net.	I tried to jump over the net.
I heard <u>ya</u> scream.	I heard you scream
Now try <u>ta</u> stand up.	Now try to stand up.
Don't plan <u>ta</u> play any more tennis.	Don't plan to play any more tennis.
It's important <u>ta</u> lie down.	It's important to lie down.
But if you <u>wanna gimme</u> a tennis lesson . . .	But if you want to give me a tennis lesson . . .

*The underlined forms are not acceptable spellings in written English.

H. You will hear a short conversation. Write the missing words.

NORIKO: I _____ _____ call you this morning. Do you

_____ _____ go out for lunch with me?

DEBBIE: No, thanks. I _____ _____ eat a big dinner tonight.

NORIKO: Yeah, but it's _____ _____ have three meals a day.

PART TWO
SUMMARIZING THE MAIN IDEAS

A. You will hear a radio report about an earthquake. What kinds of information will the report probably give you?

B. Listen again. Write four questions about the earthquake report. Use the question words below.

1. What _____ ?

2. Where _____ ?

3. When _____ ?

4. How many _____ ?

C. Listen to the report again. Answer your questions and use the answers to retell a simpler report of the earthquake.

PART THREE
MAKING INFERENCES

Listen to the following conversations about emergencies. Decide what each situation is, and circle the answer in your book. Then listen to the next part of the conversation. It gives you the correct answer.

1. a. a fire
    b. a rainstorm
    c. an earthquake

2. a. a heart attack
    b. a car breakdown
    c. a boating accident

3. a. a car breakdown
    b. a car accident
    c. an empty gas tank

4. a. The bus is late.
    b. The speakers lost their map.
    c. The speakers are lost.

5. a. an airplane accident
    b. the hijacking of an airplane
    c. the kidnapping of a child

PART FOUR

LISTENING TASKS

A. Herb goes to a clinic because his knee still hurts. In the waiting room he overhears a policeman talking to an old lady and her companion. Listen to what they tell the policeman.

Listen again. Complete the form with a description of the thief.

SUSPECT DESCRIPTION FORM

Sex: _____

Age: _____

Hair color: _____

Beard: yes   no   Moustache: yes   no

Height: _____

Weight: _____

Clothing: _____

_____

Special marks: _____

Look at the men in the police station in the drawing. With a partner, decide which man probably stole the purse. Use your suspect description form.

B. Choking is a common emergency. Listen to the following instructions; they tell how to help someone who is choking. Circle (a) or (b) to match each instruction with the correct picture.

1. **a.**   **b.**

2. **a.**   **b.**

3. a.

b.

4. a.

b.

Using the correct pictures, tell the steps to two classmates. Ask them to follow your directions. Then change roles.

PART FIVE

SPEAKING ACTIVITIES

A. Pair work. Look at the pictures. Each person is doing something wrong. With a partner, tell what not to do and why not.

Don't cross the street when the light is red. You might have an accident.

1. _____

2. _____

3. _____

4. _____

B. **Discussion.** Describe an emergency situation that you really saw or heard about. Use the past continuous tense when possible.

   Example: Last week I saw a fire. A big hotel was burning. Everyone was screaming. . . .

C. **Role play.** With a partner, act out the following emergency telephone conversations. Try to ask and answer other questions that you think are important.

STUDENT A	STUDENT B
1. Situation: Fire in apartment building.	Questions: Address? Injury? What floor? Caller's location? Instructions (what to do while waiting for help):
2. Situation: Fight between husband and wife. Husband has knife.	Questions: Address? Injury? Caller's name? What are they doing? Instructions:
3. Situation: Bank robbery across the street.	Questions: Location? Cars? Number of robbers? Injuries? Instructions:
4. Situation: Young child looks sick. Bottle of pills open nearby.	Questions: What's wrong with child? Number of pills taken? Age? Address? Kind of pills? Instructions:

Discuss Student B's instructions. Did he or she give good advice for each situation? What is the best thing to do in each situation? Your teacher may help you with this.

C. **Cartoon skits.** Teresa is taking her pregnant sister, Judy, to the hospital. On the way, however, they have a flat tire. Can Teresa fix it? Is there enough time? What will they do?

Prepare a conversation with a partner. Use expressions and idioms from this chapter. Then put on a skit about the situation.

7

HEALTH AND ILLNESS

Idioms and Useful Expressions in this Chapter

You will hear the following expressions in this chapter. If you are not sure what they mean, try to guess the meanings from the context.

to show (someone) around
to be in good shape
to get in shape
a sore throat
to take care of yourself
to get better
low-fat

sugar-free
on a diet
Ouch!
a good workout
a health food store
a checkup

PART ONE

GETTING THE MAIN IDEAS

A. Listen to the following conversation. It takes place in a health club. You may not understand every word. Listen for the main ideas.

B. Listen again. Write the following stressed words in the correct places:

weight	think	great	dancing	really
machines	use	show (twice)	right	heart
around	doesn't	do	three	
good	harder	week	like	
looks	room	exercise	instructors	

INSTRUCTOR: I _____ you're going to _____ it here. Let me

_____ you _____ . Here's the _____

_____ . Our _____ will _____ you how to _____ these _____ .

TOM: That looks _____ , doesn't it?

KENJI: Yeah.

INSTRUCTOR: And here is our _____ room.

KENJI: So, they're just _____ ?

INSTRUCTOR: Well, it _____ like it, _____ it? But they're _____ working _____ than you think.

TOM: That's very _____ for your _____ , isn't it?

INSTRUCTOR: That's _____ . You should _____ this at least _____ times a _____ if you want to be in good shape.

C. Now listen again. Repeat each sentence after the speaker. Remember that stressed words are *louder* and *clearer* than unstressed words.

D. Now listen to the rest of the conversation. Underline the stressed words.

KENJI: There're better ways to get in shape, aren't there?

INSTRUCTOR: Well, some people prefer to swim. Let me show you our pool.

TOM: Wow, that woman swims much faster than I do!

INSTRUCTOR: Oh, don't worry; that's Ellen, one of our instructors.

KENJI: I'd like to take lessons from her!

INSTRUCTOR: You're not the only one. C'mon. I'll show you the showers and the locker room. You know, I advise you to join the club before the end of the month.

KENJI: Really? Why?

INSTRUCTOR: We have a special discount for students this month. Let's go to my office. I'll tell you about it.

E. Listen again. Notice the stressed words.

F. Listen to the following questions. You will hear each question twice. Write the answers.

1. _____

2. _____

3. _____

4. _____

5. _____

6. _____

7. _____

G. Intonation. Questions at the end of sentences are called "tag questions." Affirmative statements take negative tag questions: He is strong, isn't he? Negative statements take affirmative tag questions: She isn't tired, is she? People use tag questions in two ways. Listen to the following examples. Notice the difference in intonation.

1. Your father is a doctor, <u>isn't he?</u> ↑

2. Your father is a doctor, <u>isn't he?</u> ↓

In the first example, the speaker is unsure of the answer. His voice goes up: Your father is a doctor, <u>isn't he?</u> ↑ In the second example, the speaker is almost sure the father is a doctor. <u>His voice goes down. Your father is a doctor, isn't he?</u> ↓

Repeat the following tag questions as in the first example; the voice goes up.

Repeat the following tag questions as in the second example; the voice goes down.

H. Now listen to the examples from the dialogue. From the intonation, decide if the speaker was sure or unsure of the answer. Circle the correct answer.

1. sure   unsure

2. sure   unsure

3. sure   unsure

4. sure   unsure

PART TWO

SUMMARIZING THE MAIN IDEAS

A. Barbara is at the university health service. Listen to her conversation with her doctor.

B. Listen again to the conversation and take notes.

BARBARA'S COMPLAINTS	DOCTOR'S ADVICE
1. _____	1. _____
2. _____	2. _____
3. _____	3. _____
4. _____	4. *call in a week if not better*
5. _____	
6. _____	
7. *sore throat*	

C. Now use past-tense verbs to summarize Barbara's visit to the doctor. Include all of the important information.

PART THREE

MAKING INFERENCES

A. Listen to each conversation. There is one "strange," or unusual, thing in each. Say what it is. Then listen to the next part of the conversation. It gives you the correct answer.

1. What's strange about this conversation?
2. What's strange about this conversation?
3. What's strange about this conversation?

B. Listen to the following dialogues. What are they about? Circle the correct answer.

    1. a. Nancy's having an operation.
          b. Nancy's going to have a baby.
          c. Nancy's working at the hospital.

    2. a. coffee shop
          b. supermarket
          c. health food store

PART FOUR

LISTENING TASKS

You will hear three telephone conversations about health situations. Take notes on each call.

CONVERSATION 1

Reason for call: _____

Name of dentist: _____

Time of appointment: _____

Location: _____

CONVERSATION 2

Reason for call: _____

Name of patient: _____

Price of medicine: _____

Special instructions: _____

_____

CONVERSATION 3

Reasons for call: 1. _____

                 2. _____

Time of appointments: 1. _____

                     2. _____

Name of baby's doctor: _____

Name of husband's doctor: _____

PART FIVE

SPEAKING ACTIVITIES

A. Pair work. Working with a partner, match each picture with the correct remedy. Use *should, ought to,* or *had better.*

He has a headache; he should take some aspirin.

1.

2.

3.

4.

5.

Possible Remedies

1. Drink tea.
2. Drink hot milk.
3. Put it in hot water.
4. Take a cold shower.
5. Bandage it.
6. Put ice on it.
7. Drink whiskey.
8. Take a sleeping pill.

B. Discussion. Tell the class about popular cures for common illnesses—things that a doctor doesn't necessarily tell you to do.

Examples: My grandmother thinks that chicken soup is good for a cold.
In my country we eat honey to cure a cough.

C. Role play. Create a dialogue with a partner for one of the following situations. You can use the conversations in Part Four as models.

SITUATION 1:   Call your dentist to change an appointment. Include this information: (a) time of old appointment, (b) reason for change, (c) time of new appointment.

SITUATION 2:   Make an appointment with a doctor. Include this information: (a) reason for call, (b) day you want to go in, (c) hours when the doctor can see you, (d) location of doctor's office, (e) what kind of insurance you have.

SITUATION 3:   Tell your doctor about a health problem. Include this information: (a) your symptoms, (b) when they started, (c) how often you have them, (d) doctor's orders.

Examples of symptoms: cough
fever
a pain (in my . . .)
My . . . hurts.
My . . . is sore.
dizzy
nauseous
swollen

D. Cartoon skits. Dr. Straithead, a psychiatrist, has a very interesting patient. His name is Mr. Rich, and he comes to Dr. Straithead's office every Wednesday to talk about his very unusual problem. Today, the doctor will finally tell him what to do.

Prepare a conversation with a partner. Use expressions and idioms from this chapter. Then put on a skit about the situation.

TELEVISION AND THE MEDIA

Idioms and Useful Expressions in this Chapter

You will hear the following expressions in this chapter. If you are not sure what they mean, try to guess the meanings from the context.

That's my point.
I know what you mean.
to turn into (someone or something)
the news
to drive off the road
the top story

to hit the brakes
to run out of gas(oline)
to check it out
What's on (T.V.)?
game shows
western(s)
a comedy series

PART ONE

GETTING THE MAIN IDEAS

A. Listen to the following conversation about T.V. and newspapers. You may not understand every word. Listen for the main ideas.

B. Listen again. Write the following stressed words in the correct places:

sports	programs	day	family	joking
don't	news (twice)	right	guess	tell
point	time	hate	six	
here	watch	American	terrible	
minutes	this	not	thirty	

BARBARA: Hey, listen to _____ ! The average _____
_____ watches _____ hours of T.V. a day.

MARSHA: A _____ ! You're _____ .

BARBARA: No, it says so _____ _____ in this magazine.

MARSHA: I _____ I'm _____ an average American. I usually
_____ _____ T.V. at all. Most of the
_____ are _____ .

BARBARA: Well, a lot of the programs are bad, but some are okay. And what
about the _____ and _____ ?

MARSHA: Well, yeah, I guess sports are okay. But for ＿＿＿＿＿＿ , I prefer a

good newspaper.

BARBARA: Why do you say that?

MARSHA: Well, first I ＿＿＿＿＿＿ all those commercials, and then the T.V.

news stories never ＿＿＿＿＿＿ you very much.

BARBARA: Well, they don't have enough ＿＿＿＿＿＿ to say very much in

＿＿＿＿＿＿ ＿＿＿＿＿＿ .

MARSHA: That's my ＿＿＿＿＿＿ . A newspaper has more information, and you

can read just what you want to.

C. Now listen again. Repeat each sentence after the speaker. Remember that stressed words are *louder* and *clearer* than unstressed words.

D. Listen to the rest of the conversation. Write the important words. Your notes should look like a telegram. Afterward, try to retell the conversation, using your notes.

BARBARA: *know, what, mean . . .* ＿＿＿＿＿＿＿＿＿＿＿＿＿＿＿＿

MARSHA: ＿＿＿＿＿＿＿＿＿＿＿＿＿＿＿＿＿＿＿＿＿＿＿＿

BARBARA: ＿＿＿＿＿＿＿＿＿＿＿＿＿＿＿＿＿＿＿＿＿＿＿＿

MARSHA: ＿＿＿＿＿＿＿＿＿＿＿＿＿＿＿＿＿＿＿＿＿＿＿＿

BARBARA: ＿＿＿＿＿＿＿＿＿＿＿＿＿＿＿＿＿＿＿＿＿＿＿＿

MARSHA: ＿＿＿＿＿＿＿＿＿＿＿＿＿＿＿＿＿＿＿＿＿＿＿＿

＿＿＿＿＿＿＿＿＿＿＿＿＿＿＿＿＿＿＿＿＿＿＿＿

BARBARA: ＿＿＿＿＿＿＿＿＿＿＿＿＿＿＿＿＿＿＿＿＿＿＿＿

E. Listen to the following questions. You will hear each question twice. Write the answer.

1. ＿＿＿＿＿＿＿＿＿＿＿＿＿＿＿＿＿＿＿＿＿＿＿＿

2. ＿＿＿＿＿＿＿＿＿＿＿＿＿＿＿＿＿＿＿＿＿＿＿＿

3. ＿＿＿＿＿＿＿＿＿＿＿＿＿＿＿＿＿＿＿＿＿＿＿＿

4. ＿＿＿＿＿＿＿＿＿＿＿＿＿＿＿＿＿＿＿＿＿＿＿＿

5. ＿＿＿＿＿＿＿＿＿＿＿＿＿＿＿＿＿＿＿＿＿＿＿＿

6. ＿＿＿＿＿＿＿＿＿＿＿＿＿＿＿＿＿＿＿＿＿＿＿＿

PART TWO

SUMMARIZING THE MAIN IDEAS

A. Listen to the following news report about an airplane accident. What kinds of information do you expect it to cover?

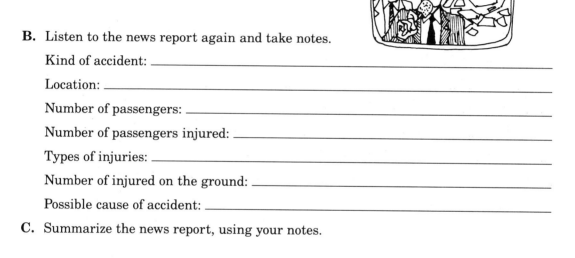

B. Listen to the news report again and take notes.

Kind of accident: _____

Location: _____

Number of passengers: _____

Number of passengers injured: _____

Types of injuries: _____

Number of injured on the ground: _____

Possible cause of accident: _____

C. Summarize the news report, using your notes.

PART THREE

MAKING INFERENCES

Listen to the following commercials. Circle the letter of the product each advertises. Then listen to the next part of the ad. It gives you the correct answer.

1. a. soup
    b. breakfast cereal
    c. vitamins

2. a. bank
    b. sleeping pill
    c. telephone company

3. a. baby products
    b. a used car
    c. a new car

4. a. breakfast food
    b. T.V. magazine
    c. sleeping pills

5. a. a magazine
    b. a T.V. drama
    c. a news program

PART FOUR

LISTENING TASKS

Marsha and her boyfriend want to watch T.V. tonight. First, look at this section from their T.V. guide. What can they watch on Channel 2 at seven-thirty? What time is the news on? On what channels? Now listen to their conversation. When you hear the pause, fill in the missing information.

TV TODAY		
WEDNESDAY		
7:30 [2]	**TWO ON THE TOWN** Beauty advice; fashion show	
[4]	_____ name of program	_____ game show/musical/news
[7]	**EYE ON THE CITY** A report on crime; a look at baby monkeys	
8 PM [13]	_____ name of program	_____ movie/sports/game show/ musical
[4] [6]	**REAL PEOPLE** Reports on a talking cow; bicycle racing; interview with recovering alcoholic	
[3]	_____ name of program	_____ western movie/comedy/sports
[ ]	_____ _____ name of program	_____ movie/interview/sports
[11]	_____ name of program	_____ game show/sports/news
8:30 [ ]	**NEWS**	
[4]	**NEWS**	
[9]	**NEWS**	
9:00 [ ]	_____ name of program	_____ sports/comedy series/news

PART FIVE

SPEAKING ACTIVITIES

A. Pair work. Tell your partner about a T.V. show you like to watch. Use this chart to organize your ideas.

Kind of show (police story, comedy, mystery, talk show, etc.):

_____

_____

_____

Type of people in it (crazy detective, single mother, etc.):

_____

_____

_____

Situation (police station in a big city, small-town coffee shop in the 1960s, etc.):

_____

_____

_____

Reason you like it (funny but not stupid, exciting, educational, etc):

_____

_____

_____

_____

Example: I like to watch the old "Kojak" show. It's about a tough policeman. He is bald, and he likes to eat candy. The policeman lives in New York and tries to catch dangerous criminals. I like the show because it's exciting and because Kojak is a smart detective . . .

B. Discussion.

1. Try to tell the story of a movie you like. Tell only the most important parts.
2. How are T.V. programs different in your country from those in the United States or Canada?
3. *Censorship* is the examination and change of material on T.V., in movies, in reading matter like books or letters, etcetera. It can be for political reasons or to exclude something the censor finds immoral, violent, or distasteful in some way. How do you feel about censorship? In what situations is censorship right or wrong? Discuss this issue. You may want to use some of these expressions to agree or disagree:

TO AGREE	TO DISAGREE
I agree.	I disagree.
I think so, too.	I don't think so.
I believe . . .	I don't believe . . .
I'm sure . . .	I'm not sure . . .
That's true (right).	That's not true (right, so).
I feel the same way.	

C. Cartoon skits. Isabella and her husband often fight about T.V. programs. Her English is not very good, and she doesn't understand most programs very well. Her husband, who is American, likes to watch the news and interview shows. Unfortunately, they only have one T.V. set.

Prepare a conversation with a partner. Use expressions and idioms from this chapter. Then put on a skit about the situation.

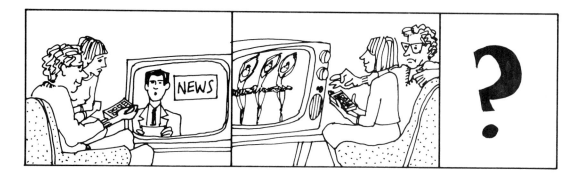

9

FRIENDS AND SOCIAL LIFE

Idioms and Useful Expressions in this Chapter

You will hear the following expressions in this chapter. If you are not sure what they mean, try to guess the meanings from the context.

What have you been up to?
No kidding!
No way.
Come on!
a blind date

a pain in the neck
live music
cover charge
a date

PART ONE

GETTING THE MAIN IDEAS

A. Herb is visiting his hometown in Texas. He meets two old friends on the street. Listen to their conversation. You may not understand every word. Listen for the main ideas.

B. Listen to the first part of the conversation again. Write the missing stressed words in the correct places.

SALLY: Jo Anne, I _____ _____ it! It's Herb Myers!

How _____ you?

HERB: Sally? Jo Anne? Wow! I haven't seen you two for over a

_____ !

JO ANNE: I _____ . You look _____ !

HERB: Thanks.

JO ANNE: What have you been _____ to?

HERB: I've been doing a _____ of things. I'm at _____

_____ .

SALLY: _____ ? That's _____ !

C. Now listen again. Repeat each sentence after the speaker. Remember that stressed words are *louder* and *clearer* than unstressed words.

D. Now listen to the rest of the conversation. Write the important words. Your notes should look like a telegram. Then retell the conversation, using your notes.

HERB: _____

JO ANNE: _____

SALLY: _____

HERB: _____

JO ANNE: _____

HERB: _____

SALLY: _____

_____

HERB: _____

JO ANNE: _____

E. Listen to the following questions. You will hear each question twice. Write the answers.

1. _____

2. _____

3. _____

4. _____

5. _____

_____

F. Intonation. In a conversation, it's important to show that you are listening and to react to the speaker or speakers. Here are some examples from the conversation of Herb, Sally, and Jo Anne. Repeat the lines after the speaker and try to copy the intonation.

G. Now listen again. Write the missing words.

Jo Anne, _____ _____ _____ _____ !

Sally? Jo Anne? _____ !

I'm at Faber College.

_____ ? _____ _____ !

What's your major— _____ ?

_____ _____ !

I have a baby _____ now.

_____ _____ !

I've been busy with my new job, selling computers. I just _____

_____ .

_____ _____ !

PART TWO

SUMMARIZING THE MAIN IDEAS

A. Listen as Sally tries to arrange a blind date for her friend Beverly. A "blind date" is an arranged date between a man and a woman who don't know each other.

B. Listen again and take notes about Franco.

Appearance: _____

Job: _____

Interests: _____

Disadvantage: _____

C. Using your notes, describe Franco.

PART THREE

MAKING INFERENCES

A. Listen to the following conversations from Larry's party. Circle the sentence that best describes each conversation. Then listen to the next part. It gives you the correct answer.

1. a. The man doesn't like the town.
   b. The man recently came to the town.
   c. The woman doesn't know the town very well.

2. a. The manager hurt his neck.
   b. The man works with the woman.
   c. The man and the woman used to work together.

3. a. The man likes to spend a lot of money.
   b. The woman doesn't really want to go out with the man.
   c. The woman likes the man very much.

4. a. The man is very worried about Tony.
   b. There are four kinds of Scotch at the party.
   c. The woman thinks Tony has been drinking too much.

5. a. The man and the woman will leave the party in forty-five minutes.
   b. The man and the woman are angry because of a misunderstanding.
   c. The woman drove the man to the party.

PART FOUR

LISTENING TASKS

Sally and Herb plan to go out over the weekend. Sally's making a few telephone calls to get some information. Think about what kind of information she needs from (1) a movie theater, (2) a nightclub, and (3) a friend giving a party. Listen to each call and take notes.

1. Name of movie theater: _____

   Location of movie theater: _____

   _____

   Name of movie: _____

   Show times: _____

   Price of tickets: _____

   Telephone number for more information: _____

2. Name of nightclub: _____

   Entertainment: _____

   Cost: _____

   Menu: _____

   Reservations: _____
              Number of people   Time   Date

3. Name of person giving party: _____

   Address: _____

   Location: _____

   Time: _____

   What to bring: _____

PART FIVE

SPEAKING ACTIVITIES

A. **Telephone practice.** Choose three real entertainment activities in your town (a movie, sporting event, dinner at a restaurant, etc.). Call to get the information you need for each activity (for example, cost, schedule, directions to get there, etc.). Report the information to the class. Use the telephone conversations in Part Four as models.

B. **Group work.** In the United States and Canada, compliments are common and accepted. People give compliments to make other people feel comfortable, to start conversations, or to be friendly.

Examples: Hon May, your English is really improving.
Excuse me. Who cut your hair? I really like it.
You really have a beautiful home, Mrs. Johnson.

To accept compliments, the common answer is "Thanks." Sometimes we answer one compliment with another.

Example: You look great, Marge.
So do you, Bob.

In small groups, practice giving and accepting compliments. Be careful not to be too personal. Here are some possible topics:

1. an item of clothing
2. a hair style
3. something someone did
4. a change someone made recently

C. **Discussion.** Discuss the following questions in small groups. Give answers for the United States and Canada, and for your own country. Ask your teacher about U.S. and Canadian customs.

1. Who pays . . .

   a. if a man and a woman are on a date?
   b. if friends go out to dinner?

2. What time should you come if you're invited to . . .

   a. dinner at eight o'clock
   b. lunch at twelve o'clock
   c. a party at eight o'clock

3. What gift should you bring . . .

    a. to a dinner party?
    b. to a party?
    c. to a birthday?
    d. to a sick friend?

D. Cartoon skits. Many people think a "dating service" is a good place to find a partner. Rose, for example, is a businesswoman and doesn't have time to look for a boyfriend. Richard, a divorced teacher, doesn't want to make a mistake again; he wants to choose the "right" woman this time. Can a dating service help them?

Prepare a conversation with a partner. Use expressions and idioms from this chapter. Then put on a skit about the situation.

10

CUSTOMS, CELEBRATIONS, AND HOLIDAYS

Idioms and Useful Expressions in this Chapter

You will hear the following expressions in this chapter. If you are not sure what they mean, try to guess the meanings from the context.

a picnic
fireworks
Trick or treat!
the bride

the groom
a honeymoon
a surprise party

PART ONE

GETTING THE MAIN IDEAS

A. Kenji is dating an American girl he met in class. He wants to buy her a gift for Valentine's Day to show her that he really likes her. What do you think you should give someone on Valentine's Day? Listen to the conversation between Kenji and a clerk at the store. You may not understand every word. Listen for the main ideas.

B. Now listen to the first part of the conversation again. Write the missing stressed words in the correct places.

CLERK: Yes, can I ＿＿＿＿＿＿＿ you with anything?

KENJI: I'm looking for a _____ gift for my _____ . Well,

actually she's not my girlfriend yet, so I really don't know

_____ to _____ her.

CLERK: How about some _____ ?

KENJI: Well, I think she's on a _____ .

CLERK: Then how about _____ her some jewelry?

KENJI: I don't want to spend _____ much money.

C. Now listen again. Repeat each sentence after the speaker. Remember that
stressed words are *louder* and *clearer* than unstressed words.

D. Listen to the second part of the conversation again. Write the important words. Your notes should look like a telegram. Afterward, try to retell the conversation, using your notes.

CLERK: *bottle cologne*

she'll like that

KENJI: *give something unusual*

CLERK: _____

_____

_____

KENJI: _____

CLERK: _____

_____

KENJI: _____

E. Listen to the following questions. You will hear each question twice. Write the answers.

1. _____

2. _____

3. _____

4. _____

5. _____

6. _____

PART TWO

SUMMARIZING THE MAIN IDEAS

A. Thanksgiving is a truly American holiday. You can learn more about it from the following conversation.

B. Listen to the conversation again and take notes.

1. Description of first Thanksgiving: _____

_____

_____

2.   Reason for Thanksgiving: _____

_____

3.   Time of year: _____

4.   Foods eaten: _____

_____

C. Now tell about Thanksgiving in your own words. Use your notes.

_____

_____

_____

_____

_____

_____

_____

PART THREE

MAKING INFERENCES

Listen to the following conversations about holidays and celebrations. Decide what each situation is. Circle the best answer in your book. Then listen to the next part of the conversation. It gives you the correct answer.

1.   a.   the president's birthday
     b.   the Fourth of July
     c.   New Year's Eve

2.   a.   Christmas
     b.   Thanksgiving
     c.   Halloween

3.   a.   Christmas
     b.   the man's birthday
     c.   Valentine's Day

4.   a.   New Year's Day
     b.   Christmas
     c.   a birthday

5.   a.   a wedding
     b.   a party
     c.   a birthday party

PART FOUR

LISTENING TASKS

A. Tom, Barbara, Herb, and Kenji are planning a surprise birthday party for Mike. Listen to their conversation.

B. Listen again. Who will do each task? Barbara, Kenji, Tom, or Herb? Write the name next to the task.

1. Inviting people: _____

2. Cleaning: _____

3. Baking the cake: _____

4. Buying drinks: _____

5. Cooking chili: _____

6. Bringing Mike to the party: _____

PART FIVE

SPEAKING ACTIVITIES

A. Discussion. Tell what is wrong with these drawings.

1.

2.

3.

Now describe some major holidays in your country. How do people celebrate them? Are there any special days for each person in your country, like birthdays in the United States and Canada (for example, saints' days or name days)?

B. Group work. Think about your next holiday or vacation. Use these verbs, plus infinitives (*to* + verb), to tell classmates about your plans: *need, plan, want, hope, would like.*

Example: Next Christmas, I plan to go to Colorado.

Continue the description of your next holiday or vacation. Use *be interested in, will enjoy, will spend* (an hour, a day, etc.) plus a gerund (-*ing* word).

Example: On New Year's Eve, I'll spend all day watching football on T.V.

C. Role play. Look at the following invitations. With a classmate, create a conversation for each invitation. One person gives the invitation. The other person *accepts* the invitation and asks a related question. Present your conversation to the class. Here are some useful expressions to invite someone to do something or to accept an invitation:

TO INVITE SOMEONE	TO ACCEPT AN INVITATION
Would you like to . . . ?	I'd be happy (delighted) to . . .
Do you want to . . . ?	Yes, I'd love to . . .
Why don't you (we) . . . ?	Sure, that sounds great!

Example: A: Can you come over for dinner tonight?
B: *Sure, I'd love to. What time* ?
A: *Around seven o'clock* .

A: I know about a Halloween party on Saturday. Do you want to go?

B: _____ . _____ ?

A: _____ .

A: What are you doing on New Year's Eve? Can you join us?

B: _____ . _____ ?

A: _____ .

A: There's a new movie at the Fox Theater. Do you want to go see it?

B: _____ . _____ ?

A: _____ .

Now *refuse* the following invitations, and give an excuse. To be polite, you should try to explain why you can't accept. You might suggest getting together another time. Here are some ways to refuse an invitation:

Example: Thanks, but I can't.
Thanks for asking, but I have other plans.
I'd love to, but I'm busy.

A: Would you like to go skiing in Switzerland with me?

B: _____ .

A: Why don't you have a cup of coffee with us?

B: _____ .

A: Do you want to go to the ball game tomorrow? I have an extra ticket.

B: _____ .

A: We're going dancing Saturday night. Would you like to come?

B: _____ .

D. Cartoon skits. Today is Carol and David's wedding day. One hundred guests are waiting for them in the church. Everyone is very excited, except Carol. She is too nervous. In fact, she doesn't want to get married at all. She has only five minutes to tell David why she's changed her mind and doesn't want to marry him.

Prepare a conversation with a partner. Use expressions and idioms from this chapter. Then put on a skit about the situation.

11

RECREATION

Idioms and Useful Expressions in this Chapter

You will hear the following expressions in this chapter. If you are not sure what they mean, try to guess the meanings from the context.

from the sixties (1960s)
a football widow
That's too bad.
in the twenties (1920s)
outdoors
travel arrangements

to go nonstop
How much do I owe you?
one way
round trip
a rec center
"you guys"

PART ONE

GETTING THE MAIN IDEAS: STRESSED WORDS

A. Herb and his older brother William are talking about folk music. Listen to their conversation and to the song they play on the record player.

B. Listen again. Write the missing stressed words in the correct places.

WILLIAM: What are you guys _____ this _____ ?

HERB: We've got _____ to a _____ . They've got

_____ _____ _____ singers from the

_____ playing.

WILLIAM: That's _____ . I used to _____ folk

_____ , but I haven't _____ to it for a

_____ _____ .

HERB: I haven't _____ . In _____ , I haven't

_____ a _____ concert since the one

_____ took me to when _____ was just a kid. I'm

_____ forward to it.

WILLIAM: Oh, yeah . . . _____ a minute. I want you to _____

something. I _____ you haven't heard _____ song

since _____ .

Where _____ all the _____ _____ ?
Long time passing.

Where _____ all the _____ _____ ?

Long time _____ .

Where have all the _____ _____ ?

The girls _____ _____ them every one.

Oh, when _____ you ever _____ ?

Oh, when _____ you ever _____ ?

Where _____ all the _____ _____ _____ ?
Long time passing.

Where _____ all the _____ _____

_____ ?
Long time ago.

Where have all the _____ _____ _____ ?

_____ _____ husbands every one.

Oh, when will you ever learn?
Oh, when will you ever learn?

Where _____ all the _____ _____

_____ ?
Long time passing.

Where _____ all the _____ _____

_____ ?
Long time ago.

Where have all the _____ _____ _____ ?

They're all in _____ .

Oh, when _____ you ever _____ ?

Oh, when _____ you ever _____ ?†

C. Now listen again. Repeat each sentence after the speaker. Remember that stressed words are *louder* and *clearer* than unstressed words.

D. Listen to the following questions. You will hear each question twice. Write the answers.

1. _____
2. _____
3. _____
4. _____
5. _____
6. _____
   _____
   _____

PART TWO

SUMMARIZING THE MAIN IDEAS

A. You'll hear a brief lecture on American football. What do you know about this sport? What do the players look like? Have you ever seen an American football game? As you listen, you might try to compare it to football or soccer in your country.

B. Listen to the talk again and take notes.

Football season: _____

Kinds of teams: _____

Uniforms (clothing): _____

Object (goal) of game: _____

"Pro" (professional) players: _____

Games on T.V.: _____

C. Describe American football, using your notes.

PART THREE

MAKING INFERENCES

Listen to the following conversations about recreational activities. Circle the answer to each question you hear. Then listen to the next part of the conversation. It gives you the correct answer.

1. a. to a disco
   b. to a concert
   c. to a party

2. a. chess
   b. checkers
   c. baseball

3. a. took a short trip
   b. visited her grandmother
   c. relaxed at home

4. a. to the movies
   b. to an art museum
   c. to an Indian village

5. a. having a picnic at the beach
   b. cooking in the kitchen
   c. having lunch at a restaurant

PART FOUR

LISTENING TASKS

A. People travel for different reasons. Think of the trips you've made or would like to make. What kind of plans do you have to make before a trip? You will hear some conversations about people making travel arrangements. Listen to each conversation and take notes.

1. Reason for trip: _____

   Destination: _____
                                       country   city

   Date of departure: _____

   Date of return: _____

   Plane change: _____

   Cost of ticket: _____

   Class of ticket: _____

2. Reason for trip: _____

   Destination: _____

   Departure: _____   _____
             (time)   (day)

   Arrival: _____   _____
           (time)   (day)

   Cost of ticket: _____

   Date of return: _____

3. Reason for trip: _____

   Destination: _____

   Size of car: _____

   Cost per week: _____

   Special features: _____

   Place to pick car up: _____

B. A few of Herb's high-school friends are visiting the college campus. They're surprised at the number of interesting things to do there. Listen as Herb shows them where to go for fun. Look at the map of campus as you listen.

   Now listen again. On the map, write the activities or attractions in the correct place.

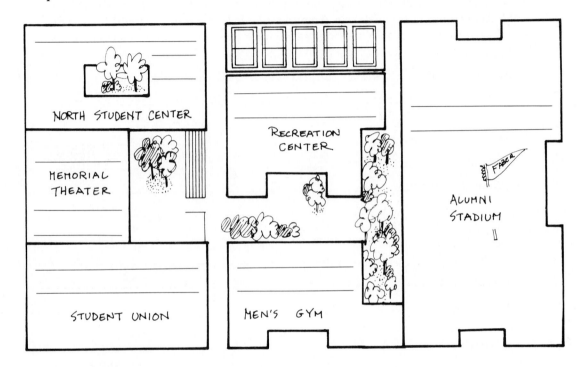

PART FIVE

SPEAKING ACTIVITIES

A. Telephone practice. Call an airline or a travel agent and, in English, get some information about flying from your city to (1) Chicago, (2) Seattle, (3) New York, (4) Dallas, (5) Vancouver, (6) your home country. Make sure you ask about costs, travel time, transfers, discounts, and special conditions (for example, having to pay seven days before the flight). Share your information with your classmates. See who found the least expensive flight.

B. Pair work. With a partner, plan a short trip to your home country or city. Make a list of places to see and things to do. Make recommendations about how much money to take, what kind of clothing to wear, how to get around, and so forth. Include any advice a visitor would need.

C. Group work. Describe a game or sport that you know. Include information about the number of players, the basic rules, any special clothing or other equipment you need, and where to play.

D. Cartoon skits. Tony Cordova is overworked and needs a vacation. His travel agent is trying to suggest some places, but it's not easy: Tony is very picky. He has already been to many countries and he wants to go someplace where he has never been. He doesn't want to spend too much money.

Prepare a conversation with a partner. Use expressions and idioms from this chapter. Then put on a skit about the situation.

12

YOU, THE CONSUMER

Idioms and Useful Expressions in this Chapter

*You will hear the following expressions in this chapter. If you are not
sure what they mean, try to guess the meanings from the context.*

Oh, darn
a car dealer
a queen-size bed
to shoot (a picture)
built-in
frost-free
dirt-cheap
remote control
to test-drive

It's ridiculous!
Calm down!
to take the charges off the bill
Yuk!
under warranty
best offer
garage sale
bargaining
to make an offer

PART ONE

GETTING THE MAIN IDEAS

A. Marsha often shops in large department stores. Listen to the following conversation. You may not understand every word. Listen for the main ideas. Did
anything like this ever happen to you?

B. Listen again. Write the missing stressed words in the correct places.

MAN: Miss! Do you think I could _____ some _____
here?

SALESWOMAN: Certainly, sir. I'll be _____ _____ .

MAN: I've already been _____ here for _____

_____ , you know.

MARSHA: I believe _____ was here _____ .

SALESWOMAN: All right. What can I _____ you with?

MARSHA: I'm interested in your _____ .

MAN: I'd like to see some _____ .

SALESWOMAN: Well, that makes it _____ . Why don't you _____

take a look at what we've _____ . These are our designer

ties. They're _____ _____ _____ .

MARSHA: Are they all _____ ?

SALESWOMAN: Uh-huh.

MAN: Oh, I think I like this _____ one in _____ .

MARSHA: Uh-huh. That's really gorgeous. It'll look _____ on you.

C. Now listen again. Repeat each sentence after the speaker. Remember that stressed words are *louder* and *clearer* than unstressed words.

D. Listen to the rest of the conversation and write the important words. Your notes should look like a telegram. Afterward, try to reconstruct the conversation, using your notes.

MAN: _____

MARSHA: _____

_____

MAN: _____

SALESWOMAN: _____

MARSHA: _____

MAN: _____

_____

MARSHA: _____

_____

E. Listen to the following questions. You will hear each question twice. Write the answers.

1. _____
2. _____
3. _____
4. _____
5. _____
6. _____
7. _____

PART TWO

SUMMARIZING THE MAIN IDEAS

A. Herb is interested in buying a used car. On the radio, he hears a show offering advice on this subject. Have you ever bought a used car? What are some important things to think about before you buy one? Listen to the radio report Herb hears.

B. Listen to the radio program again and take notes. Don't try to copy whole sentences. Just write the important information.

_____

_____

_____

_____

_____

_____

C. Listen again until you can organize your notes into the following short outline:

I.   Introduction

_____

_____

II.   Places to buy

    A. _____

        1. Advantage(s): _____

        2. Disadvantage(s): _____

    B. _____

        1. Advantage(s): _____

        2. Disadvantage(s): _____

        3. Questions to ask: _____

_____

D. Now summarize the information in the radio lecture. Use your outline and notes.

PART THREE

MAKING INFERENCES

Listen to these people and their complaints. Circle the answer to each question you hear. Then listen to the next part of the conversation. It gives you the correct answer.

1. a. a radio
   b. a battery
   c. a watch

2. a. his credit card bill
   b. his telephone bill
   c. his airline bill

3. a. spoiled milk
   b. rotten eggs
   c. spoiled meat

4. a. to the painter
   b. to the tailor
   c. to the hairdresser

5. a. The customer will probably find her receipt.
   b. The customer will probably get her money back.
   c. The customer will probably decide to exchange the gift.

6. a. for the repair work
   b. for the broken parts
   c. for the new T.V. set

PART FOUR

LISTENING TASKS

A. Now, at the end of the school year, Tom and Kenji are renting an apartment for the summer. They are interested in buying a few things. Match the telephone conversation you hear with the correct newspaper ad: Circle (a), (b), or (c). As you listen, underline the information in the ad that you hear about in the conversation.

1. a.

   Sears fridge—works like new. Great for apartments, dorms. Only $100, firm. Call 555-5313.

   b.

   White, bar-sized refrig. Brand new w/warranty. Must sell—$150 or best offer. Call eves: 555-2341.

   c.

   Family size refrig. Brown w/ ice maker. Excell. cond. Reasonably priced. Call Mary: 555-1111.

2. a.

Japanese 10-speed bike. Perfect shape—used only twice by pro racer. $275 o.b.o. Call 555-1910.

   b.

Lady's 10-speed, 26-inch frame, new tires. Must sell—leaving country. Needs minor repair. Call 555-4988.

   c.

Two great bikes! Men's 10-speed—Schwinn, Lady's 3-speed—Huffy. Each $150 new. Will sell CHEAP! Tel: 555-6789.

3. a.

19″ RCA color T.V.—won on T.V. game show. $300. Call 555-2565.

   b.

1977 RCA color console. New picture tube. Works like new. $200. Call 555-4567.

   c.

Almost-new hotel T.V.s at great discount! 90-day guarantee. Call 555-5780.

4. a.

Garage sale. All my furniture must go: chairs, tables, couch, office desk, and much more. Come early Sat. A.M. for best selection. Tel: 555-9999.

   b.

Modern Danish desk. All wood, great for office or home. $175. Call Saturday: 555-0000.

   c.

Office furn. clearance! All desks must go—cheap. Filing cabinets 20% off. Call for prices 9–5: 555-4588.

B. Look at the picture of the department store. It shows the location of the departments on the second floor. Each department is numbered. You will hear someone give directions on how to get from one part of the store to another. As you listen, follow the directions so that you can write the name of the destination next to the number of the destination on the map. There are four parts to this exercise.

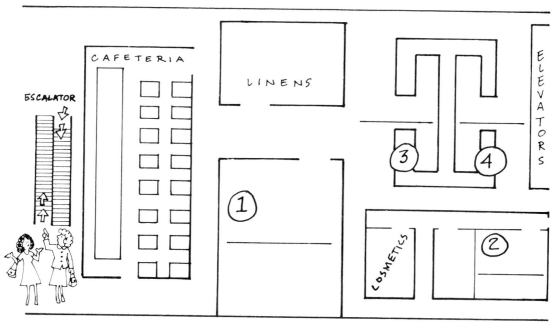

Listen to each set of directions again. Then check your answer.

PART FIVE

SPEAKING ACTIVITIES

A. Phone assignments. Collect some ads from local newspapers for things you might be interested in buying. (You may have to ask your teacher for help with this.) After reading an ad carefully, make a list of questions you would need to ask the seller. Then call the seller (person or store) and ask as many questions as you can to get more information. (Or your teacher may ask you to play the role of the buyer and ask someone in your class to play the role of the seller.)

BUYER

To ask about the price.
   So how much is (was) it?
   How much do you want?
To make an offer or try to lower the price:
   Is that as low as you'll go?
   Is that your best (lowest) price?
   Will you take any less?

   Will you take _____ dollars?

   _____ dollars is all I can afford.

   How about _____ dollars?
To conclude:
   I'll take it.
   Let me think about it.
   Thanks anyway, but . . .

SELLER

To describe the price:
   It's a fair (reasonable) price.
   It's a bargain.
   It's a great deal (a steal).
To hold the price:
   That's the best I can do.
   The price is firm.
   Take it or leave it.
To be more flexible:
   I might take a little less.
   Make me an offer.
To conclude:
   Well, do you want it?
   So, what do you think?
   I'm sure you'll like it.

1. Play the roles of Tom or Kenji and the seller of the items in Part Four (the refrigerator, the bicycle, the television, and the desk). The buyer (Tom or Kenji) goes to the seller's home to try to buy each of the items. Use the expressions above in Exercise B. Try to agree on a fair price.

2. In Part Three, you heard customers complaining about something they bought or about some service. With a classmate, play the roles of an unsatisfied customer and a salesclerk or a store manager. Describe the problem and decide if you want an exchange, a refund, or a reduced charge. (Examples of problems: squeaky mattress, broken toy, incorrect phone bill, broken microwave oven, scratched table, broken dress zipper, etc.)

C. **Cartoon skits.** Andrea has always respected elderly people. But one day she sees something strange at a department store. A lady, old enough to be her grandmother, is shoplifting. Andrea could talk to her, or she could call the manager, or . . .

Prepare a conversation with a partner. Use expressions and idioms from this chapter. Then put on a skit about the situation.